Supplies

PAINTS

Paints used are DecoArt™ Americana® Acrylics and DecoArt™ JansenArt™ Traditions Acrylics. Please refer to individual projects for specific palettes.

BRUSHES

LOEW CORNELL®
LA CORNEILLE® GOLDEN TAKLON
Series 7000 Round: #1, #2, #3, #5
Series 7300 Shader (flat): #4, #6, #8, #10, #12, #20
Series 7350 Liner: #10/0, #1
NATURAL BRISTLE
Series 1136 Stencil: #8 (for stenciling and splattering)
MISCELLANEOUS
Series 1178 Wash: 1 1/2"
Worn bristle round: #6 (for drybrushing)

BASIC SUPPLIES

Brown paper bags
DecoArt Faux Glazing Medium™ (DS18) or DecoArt
    JansenArt Traditions Glazing Medium (JAM01)
Lint-free cotton cloths
Palette paper

Paper towels
Pencil (for tracing)
Sandpaper, 400-grit
Saral Transfer Paper, blue and white
Stylus
Tape (for securing traced patterns)
Tracing paper
Varnishes: DecoArt Americana Gloss Varnish (DS13), DecoArt
    JansenArt Traditions Satin Varnish (JAM04) or DecoArt
    Americana Acrylic Sealer/Finisher (DAS12)
Water basin
Wood sealer: DecoArt Multi-Purpose Sealer (DS17) or
    DecoArt JansenArt Traditions Multi-Surface Sealer (JAM03)

Please refer to the individual projects for special supplies.

Source

Laura Craft Studio
Web site: www.pinturadecorativa.com/lauracraft.html
E-mail: lauracraft@pinturadecorativa.com

Contents

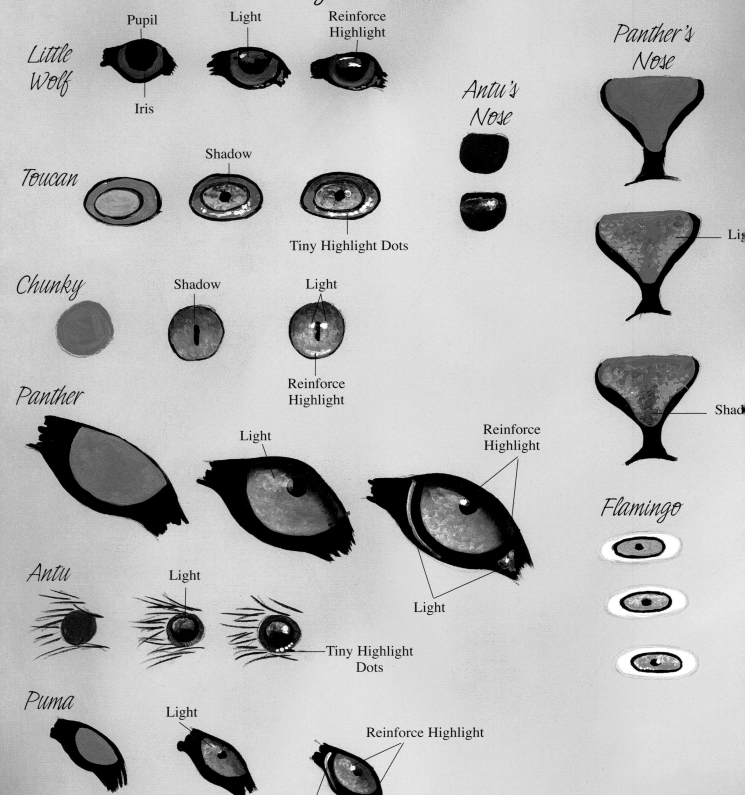

Little Wolf

Pupil
Light
Reinforce Highlight
Iris

Toucan

Shadow
Tiny Highlight Dots

Antu's Nose

Panther's Nose

Chunky

Shadow
Light
Reinforce Highlight

Panther

Light
Reinforce Highlight
Light

Antu

Light
Tiny Highlight Dots

Flamingo

Puma

Light
Reinforce Highlight
Light

SURFACE PREPARATION

WOOD: Sand thoroughly with #400-grit sandpaper until smooth. Wipe with a cotton cloth to remove the dust. Seal the surface with wood sealer. When dry, lightly sand again, if necessary, to remove any raised grain, then wipe to remove dust.

MDF BOARD: Seal with wood sealer. Lightly sand to remove any roughness, then wipe to remove dust.

CANVAS: Primed canvas needs no preparation.

BASECOATING

Use the wash brush to basecoat backgrounds. Apply two coats of paint, allowing the first coat to dry before applying the second. Once the second coat is dry, lightly sand with a piece of brown paper bag. Wipe the surface with a soft cotton cloth to remove the dust.

TRANSFERRING THE PATTERN

Trace the pattern onto tracing paper. Center the traced pattern on the surface and tape it down. Place your transfer paper under the traced pattern (with the coated side down) and transfer the basic outlines with a stylus, omitting the details for now. Transfer the details as needed, but don't transfer the lines for the hair.

PAINT CONSISTENCY

Use the acrylics straight from the bottle, except for the following techniques:

LINEWORK: Add enough water to the paint so it has the consistency of ink.

MOTTLING: Add enough water to the paint so it has the consistency of ink. The paint must be thin enough to drip from the brush to the surface.

WASH: Add two parts of water to one part of paint (2:1).

PAINTING LAYERS

Unless specifically stated otherwise in the instructions for a project or technique, allow each layer of paint to dry thoroughly before painting another layer.

FINISHING

Once you have finished your work, allow the paint to dry thoroughly.

SPRAY VARNISH: Hold the can about 8" from the surface and spray your project. Allow to dry, then sand with a fine-grit sandpaper or piece of brown paper bag. Wipe to remove dust. Apply two or three layers of varnish in this manner.

WATERBASED VARNISH: Use a 1 1/2" wash brush to apply several layers of varnish. Allow each layer to dry, then sand and remove the dust with a soft cloth before applying the next layer.

Techniques

CRISSCROSS STROKES

This technique is used to create a background with multiple colors. First basecoat the surface with white using a 1 1/2" wash brush. Allow to dry. Using a #12 flat brush (or appropriate size to fit the area), apply three or more colors in sequence (side by side) on your surface. Since no retarder or blending medium is used, you must work quickly and in one small area at a time so that the paint does not dry before the colors are blended. Next, use your flat brush to work the colors together, stroking with a random, crisscross motion (like painting X's) in all directions. You want a smooth background in which the colors are slightly blended together. Repeat the procedure until you have completely covered the surface. The final result should be a blurred background showing several colors.

DRYBRUSH

This technique is used for highlighting or adding light reflection. Load a dry brush (I use a worn #6 round bristle brush) with a small amount of paint. Remove excess paint by wiping the brush on a paper towel, then apply lightly and smoothly to the surface using a circular motion.

FLOATING

The floating technique is often used to paint the highlights and the shadows on a project.

Dip your flat brush into water, then blot excess water from the brush by lightly laying the flat side on a paper towel. Load one corner of the brush with paint and stroke on your palette to work the color across the brush, almost to the other side. The result should be a smooth transition of color that is stronger on the loaded side and gradually fades to clear water on the opposite side of the brush. Apply to your project.

MOTTLING

Mottling is a two-step process that uses the wicking action of water to spread paint in a random fashion.

Basecoat the area as directed. Allow to dry. Use a very wet brush to pick up the thinned paint to be used for mottling. Drip this randomly over the surface. While the first dripped color is wet, repeat with a second color. You may also work with a third color.

Each successive color will spread softly, giving a mottled effect.

LIGHT REFLECTION

Remember to allow each layer to dry before applying the next layer. Load the stiff, dry brush with a very small amount of the highlight color, then wipe off most of the paint on a paper towel. Using as little pressure as possible and a circular

(Continued on Page 6)

Techniques
(Continued from Page 5)

motion, drybrush paint on the highlight area. Load the brush with Titanium White, then apply to the highlight area, this time covering a smaller area. Finally, use the liner brush and Titanium White to add an extra-bright spot to the highlight area.

PAINTING EYES AND NOSES

Each animal has distinctive features. When painting eyes and noses, please refer to the Eyes and Noses Color Worksheet.

PAINTING FEATHERS

Feather detail consists of thin, irregular lines that follow the direction of growth as indicated in the pattern. Use the liner brush and thinned paint. Load the brush, then pull it across your palette, rolling it as you pull, to remove excess paint and to bring the tip of the brush to a point. Blot excess paint by touching the tip to a paper towel.

Place the brush on the surface, then slide the stroke toward you and lift. For longer feathers, simply pull the stroke a bit longer. Allow the surface to dry between layers.

PAINTING HAIR

When painting individual hairs, load the liner brush as for the feathers and bring the tip to a point. Blot excess paint by touching the tip to a paper towel.

Follow the direction of the strokes as indicated by arrows on the pattern. Start each stroke by pressing lightly on the surface, then smoothly slide and lift. Gradually releasing pressure on the brush allows the bristles of the brush to return to a point.

The hair is applied in layers. Allow each layer of hair to dry before painting another layer. The first layer is usually the basecoat color of the animal + a lighter value. Each successive layer is lighter in value than the last; the final layer is painted with Titanium White.

Using the drybrush technique, reinforce the light areas with Titanium White and the shadow areas with the color indicated in the directions. Don't completely cover the previous layers.

The longer hair is painted with a liner brush after you have finished painting the layers of short hair.

POUNCING

Pouncing adds texture. It is usually applied to a dry surface, using a different color than the background. Position the brush perpendicular to the surface, and then tap the brush on the surface using an up-and-down motion. For the projects in this book, I pounce with a round brush, but pouncing can be done with any brush.

SOFTEN

To blur an application of paint so that it blends into the background color, soften the edges of the wet paint by lightly brushing them with the tip of the brush. The color should look slightly smudged.

SPLATTERING

Load a dry stencil brush with paint. Hold the brush parallel to the surface, then pull the edge of the palette knife across the bristles up and toward yourself, splattering the surface with color. Test this technique on a piece of paper before applying it to your project. The closer the brush is to the surface, the bigger the splatter dots will be.

WASH

A wash is a transparent layer of paint that has been thinned with water or medium and applied over a dry surface. It is used to achieve depth in your work. It is also used to enhance highlights, and to paint shadows and reflections.

Dampen the selected area with water or glazing medium. Load the flat brush with a small amount of the wash color and apply it to the dampened area. You should be able to see the basecoat color underneath the wash.

Bird and Orange
Pages 7-9

Mabel Blanco

Basecoat

Orange

Paint feathers
on black areas

Place a dot in the lightest
area, then paint small
strokes around the dot

Begin painting
feathers on
yellow areas

Float
shading

Eyes

1st layer of
feathers

Stem
end

2nd layer of feathers

PALETTE

DECOART
AMERICANA
ACRYLICS
Antique Gold
Burnt Sienna
Burnt Umber
Cadmium Yellow
Lamp (Ebony) Black
Lemon Yellow
Mistletoe
Moon Yellow
Raw Sienna
Tangerine
Titanium White

SURFACE

Box for wooden
    spoons, design area is 7" x 8" (18 x 23 cm)

Bird and Orange

BRUSHES

Liner: #10/0
Round: #1, #3
Shader: #4, #6, #8, #10, #20

SURFACE PREPARATION

Please refer to "Surface Preparation" at the front of the book. Using the #20 flat brush, basecoat the outside of the box with Titanium White. Paint the inside and edge of the base with Moon Yellow. Allow to dry, then transfer the patterns.

PAINTING INSTRUCTIONS

Please refer to the Color Worksheet.

BACKGROUND

Please refer to "Crisscross Strokes" at the front of the book. Using crisscross strokes and the #10 flat brush, paint the background with Mistletoe and Lamp Black. Work in more Lamp Black in the corners than in other areas.

TRUNK

Basecoat the trunk with #10 flat brush and Burnt Sienna. Let dry. Use a #3 round brush to pounce Lamp Black on the lower section of the trunk. (Pounce the same color on the lower, darkest section of the orange also.)

Working with the chisel edge of the #8 flat brush and thinned Burnt Umber, paint the dark areas of the bark. Paint additional irregular strokes to highlight the raised edges of the bark with the #3 round brush and Moon Yellow.

Use Antique Gold + Titanium White (1:1) to highlight the upper part of the trunk; paint a few strokes on the rest of the trunk, avoiding the shadow areas. Use Lamp Black to paint the very darkest shadows and to touch up the dark area where the orange is pierced by the branch. Shade next to the toes with Burnt Umber.

ORANGES

Mix Tangerine + Lemon Yellow + Burnt Sienna (4:2:1) and use the #6 flat brush to basecoat the oranges.

Place a Titanium White dot on the upper part (lightest area) of the orange. Add a touch of Lemon Yellow to Titanium White, thin the mix, then paint small strokes with the liner brush, around the dot, following the shape of the orange. As you paint outward from the brightest highlight (the dot), make the lines softer and more separate from each other. After you've painted lines on about a third of the orange, add another touch of Lemon Yellow to the mix and continue painting lines.

Use the #10 flat brush to float Burnt Umber + Tangerine (1: touch) on the shadow area of the orange. Use the liner brush and thinned Burnt Umber to paint the blemish lines on the orange (refer to photo).

Using a #3 round brush loaded in Cadmium Yellow, paint the flesh of the orange that has been cut open (on front), then highlight with touches of Titanium White.

STEM ENDS (Oranges on Back Side): In the area around the stem, paint dots with thinned Tangerine and Moon Yellow, using the tip of the #3 round brush. Add a touch of Titanium White to the Moon Yellow to paint a few dots.

Use the liner brush and thinned Burnt Umber to paint the depressions and area around stem. Mix Mistletoe + Lamp Black (1: touch), then use a #4 flat brush to float color along the edges of the depressions and on the shaded area. Use Mistletoe to paint the stem ends. Add a dot to the center of the stem end with Lemon Yellow + Titanium White (1: touch).

Float shading under the oranges (on back) using a #10 flat brush and Burnt Umber.

BIRD

Using the #6 flat brush and Lamp Black, basecoat the head, throat, top of breast, legs and toes, and the black areas of the wing and tail feathers. Basecoat the yellow areas with Lemon Yellow.

Refer to "Painting Feathers" in the General Instructions. Use thinned Titanium White + Lamp Black (1: touch) and the liner brush to paint the small feathers on the head, top of chest, the primary wing feather and the black tail feathers.

Load the liner brush with thinned Tangerine to paint several layers of feathers on the breast, heaviest on the left side and fading out toward the right, following the shape of the bird.

Use thinned Lemon Yellow + Titanium White (1: touch) and the liner brush to paint several layers of feathers on the right side of the breast and around the wing. Basecoat the remaining tail feathers with the same color. The more layers of feathers that you paint, the more realistic the bird will appear. Apply a small wash of Tangerine on the larger yellow tail feather. Drybrush Burnt Umber along the belly.

Paint the details on the lower part of the wing with Titanium White and the #3 round brush.

BEAK: Basecoat the beak with Titanium White + Lamp Black (3:1).

Float Lamp Black on the lower section and Titanium White on the upper section to create a separation line between the sections. Paint a small Titanium White highlight line at the tip of the beak, just above the separation line.

EYE: Mix Titanium White + Lamp Black (3:1) and paint a circle for the eye using the #3 round brush. Now paint a smaller circle inside the first one with Lamp Black. Add several tiny Titanium White highlight dots along the bottom edge of the eye and one dot in the upper, left corner.

LEGS: Mix Titanium White + Lamp Black (1: touch) and thin; use this to highlight the rounded areas of the legs and feet. Paint a line of Titanium White on the right side of each leg and on the left side of each toe.

FINISHING

For varnishing instructions, refer to "Finishing" at the front of the book.

Bird and Orange

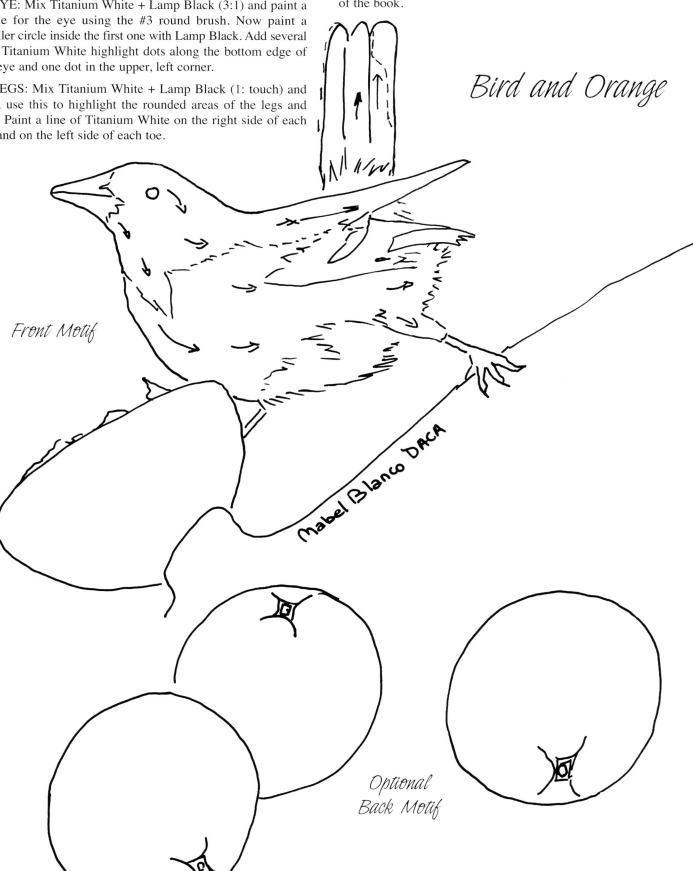

Front Motif

Mabel Blanco DACA

Optional Back Motif

Color Photo on Page 11

Antu

PALETTE
DECOART
AMERICANA
ACRYLICS
Light Buttermilk
JANSENART
TRADITIONS
ACRYLICS
Burnt Sienna
Burnt Umber
Carbon Black
Chrome Green Hue
Indian Yellow
Napthol Red
Perinone Orange
Raw Sienna
Raw Umber
Titanium White
Ultramarine Blue

SURFACE
MDF photo album, 13" x 13" (33 x 33 cm)

BRUSHES
Liner: #10/0
Round: #3
Shader: #4, #8, #12
Wash: 1 1/2"
Worn bristle round: #6

SURFACE PREPARATION
Refer to "Surface Preparation" in the front of the book. Basecoat the design area with Titanium White. Basecoat the rest of the outside of the album with Light Buttermilk and the inside with Carbon Black. Allow to dry, then transfer the pattern.

PAINTING INSTRUCTIONS
BACKGROUND
Please refer to "Crisscross Strokes" at the front of the book. Using crisscross strokes and the #12 flat brush, paint the background above the table and behind the dog with Titanium White and Ultramarine Blue. The background is a little darker behind the dog and oranges; add a little more Ultramarine Blue in these areas.

TABLECLOTH
The tablecloth has already been basecoated white. Mix Titanium White + Burnt Umber + Carbon Black (3:1: touch) and paint the tablecloth again, using the #12 flat brush.

The light will reflect with greater intensity on the top of the folds. Use Titanium White to drybrush the highlights in front of the oranges, in front and to the left of the bowl, on the top of the folds, above and below the edge of the table, and on the crease lines where the cloth had been folded.

Drybrush Burnt Umber in the shadow areas on the left side of the tablecloth, to the right of and below the oranges, below the right side of the bowl, lightly next to the crease lines cause by the folding, and on both sides of the folds.

Mix the basecoat color of the tablecloth + Carbon Black (1: touch), then drybrush the shadows from the oranges and bowl on the tablecloth.

ORANGES
Using a #8 flat brush, basecoat the oranges with Indian Yellow. Allow to dry, then use the tip of the round brush and thinned Perinone Orange to paint the dots (bumpy flesh) on the oranges.

In the area around the stem, paint dots with thinned Perinone Orange and Indian Yellow, using the tip of the round brush.

Using Perinone Orange + Titanium White (1: touch), add dots to highlight the folds around the stem area and the area near the center of the orange. The lightest dots on these areas are Titanium White.

Use the liner brush and thinned Burnt Umber to paint the stem area and depressions. Mix Chrome Green Hue + Carbon Black (1: touch), then use a #4 flat brush to float color along the edges of depressions. Use Burnt Umber + Titanium White (1:1) to paint the stem end.

Using the #8 flat brush, roughly float Burnt Umber around the outer portions of the oranges, excluding the top, right section of the two whole oranges; let dry, then repeat to reinforce the shadows.

BOWL
Using the #8 flat brush, basecoat the bowl with Titanium White + Carbon Black + Raw Umber (1: touch: touch).

Paint the strokework on the right side of the bowl using the round brush and slightly thinned Ultramarine Blue. Add a bit more water to the paint, then paint the remaining strokework.

Drybrush the bowl basecoat color + Carbon Black (1: touch) on both sides of the bowl and base, under the napkin and under the dog's paw. Outline the bottom of the base with Carbon Black.

Drybrush Titanium White highlights down the center of the bowl and on the center of the base.

NAPKIN
Using the #8 flat brush, basecoat the napkin with Titanium White, if needed. Paint the border with Napthol Red. Allow to dry, then paint a Carbon Black shadow line on the bowl, under the red border of the napkin.

Drybrush Titanium White + Carbon Black (1: touch) in the folds and on the part of the napkin inside the bowl. Allow to dry, then repeat to reinforce the shading in the bowl.

ANTU
Using the #4 flat brush and Carbon Black, basecoat top of the head, the lower part of the forehead (between the eyes), ears, both sides of the face and muzzle, along the neck and the dog's left shoulder.

Use the same brush and Titanium White + Carbon Black (1: touch) to basecoat the chest, leg, paws, middle of the forehead,

(Continued on Page 12)

Mabel Blanco

Antü

Pages 10 & 12-13

Antu
(Continued from Page 10)

chin, rest of the muzzle and the left side of the dog's face next to the muzzle.

EYES: Refer to Eyes and Noses Color Worksheet. Outline the eyes with Titanium White + Carbon Black (3:2). Use the round brush and Burnt Umber to basecoat the eyes, then paint the pupils Carbon Black. Use the liner brush and thinned Titanium White to paint a comma stroke highlight in the upper, right section of each eye, then soften. Let dry, then reinforce the highlight with a dot of Titanium White. Use the tip of the liner brush to add some dots of Titanium White on the lower, outer corner of each iris.

HAIR: You will need to paint several layers of hair to achieve a natural look. The hair growth follows the shape of the animal; refer to the arrows on the pattern. The hair on the chest, leg and paws is longer and uneven. Use the liner brush and thinned Burnt Umber to paint hair on the front of the ears, above and on the sides of the eyes, on the leg and paws, and on the chin; add a few hairs to the chest.

In the same way, use Titanium White to paint hair on the forehead, on the sides of the face, around the nose, on the chest, below the mouth, on the paws and leg, a few hairs above and under the eyes, and on the ears. Add strokes of Burnt Sienna on the paws. Add strokes of Raw Sienna on the light areas, and on the ears.

Use Carbon Black to paint hair along the top of the head, on the ears, on dark area between eyes into the white area, down the sides of the face, on the sides of the muzzle, around the neck and on the dog's left shoulder.

Use Burnt Umber to paint a few stray strands of hair around the nose.

NOSE AND MOUTH: Using the #4 flat brush, basecoat the nose with Carbon Black. Let dry. Using the round brush and thinned Titanium White, paint short strokes to highlight the tip of the nose.

Use a liner brush and Carbon Black to outline the mouth. When dry, float Raw Sienna around the nose and under the mouth.

FINISHING

Varnish following the instructions for "Finishing" in the front of the book. Use a lace or ribbon in a matching color to attach the album pieces together.

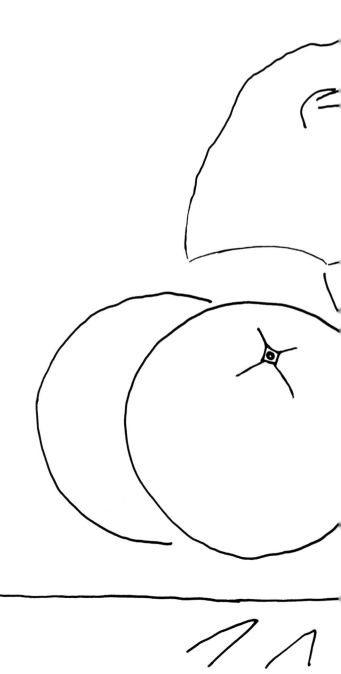

Antu

Mabel Blanco DACA

Cactus and Woodpecker

Pages 15-16

Color Photo on Page 14

PALETTE

JANSENART
TRADITIONS
ACRYLICS
Burnt Sienna
Burnt Umber
Carbon Black
Chrome Green Hue
Hansa Yellow
Lamp (Ebony) Black
Light Grey Value 8
Medium Grey
Napthol Red
Perinone Orange
Phthalo Green
Raw Sienna
Titanium White
Yellow Oxide

Cactus and Woodpecker

SURFACE

Frame to fit panel
MDF panel, 8 1/2" x 11" (20.5 x 27 cm)

BRUSHES

Liner: #10/0
Round: #1, #3
Shader: #4, #6, #8, #10, #20
Wash: 1 1/2"
Worn bristle round: #6

SURFACE PREPARATION

Please refer to "Surface Preparation" at the front of the book. Basecoat the panel with Titanium White. Allow to dry, then transfer the basic outlines of the pattern; transfer the details as you need them.

PAINTING INSTRUCTIONS

BACKGROUND

Please refer to "Crisscross Strokes" at the front of the book. Using crisscross strokes and the #20 flat brush, paint the green background with Chrome Green Hue, Yellow Oxide and Burnt Sienna. Apply a touch of Carbon Black next to the cactus.

TREE TRUNK

Please refer to the color photo when painting the tree trunk.

Using the #8 flat brush and Light Grey, basecoat the trunk and let dry. Use a #1 round brush and Carbon Black to paint the crevices of the trunk and to outline the hole.

Basecoat the interior of the hole using the #6 flat brush and Burnt Umber. Basecoat the edge of the opening with Burnt Sienna. As you paint the surface of the trunk, use a few of those colors to add detail to the edge of the opening.

Work the surface of the trunk using the chisel edge of the #8 flat brush and thinned paint. Using an up-and-down motion, apply strokes to "draw" veins in the wood. The colors should be applied randomly to create texture where the light and dark areas occur. Start painting the wood grain with Raw Sienna. Allow to dry, then repeat, first with Light Grey, and then with Medium Grey.

In the same manner, use Carbon Black to shade the left side and toward the bottom. On the right side and next to the hole, use Light Grey + Titanium White (1: touch) for highlighting.

BIRD

Using the #4 flat brush, basecoat the back, wing, tail and beak with Carbon Black.

Basecoat the area above the beak and the orange spot on the back of the head with Perinone Orange. Basecoat the red spot on the top of the head with Napthol Red and the rest of the head and body with Light Grey.

Drybrush Titanium White + Lamp Black (1: touch) under the beak, under the eye and on the cheek area. Use the #10 flat brush to float this mix around the eye.

Please refer to "Painting Feathers" in the front of the book.

Paint the small groups of feathers on the wing and the back of the bird with Titanium White; paint small semicircular rows to give shape to the bird. The strokes are short and irregular. Add a few scattered feathers as well.

Add a touch of Titanium White to Carbon Black, then paint feathers on the tip of the wing. Paint the feathers on the black tail sections with Carbon Black. On the gray areas, paint several layers of feathers with Titanium White.

On the orange spot on the back of the head, paint one layer of feathers with Hansa Yellow; allow to dry, then paint a layer with Perinone Orange + Napthol Red (1: touch). Paint the area by the beak the same way. The feathers on the red area are Perinone Orange.

BEAK: Use the #4 flat brush to float Titanium White on the upper half of the beak, creating a clear distinction between the upper and lower sections. Paint tiny Titanium White + Carbon Black (1: touch) feathers under the beak.

EYE: Basecoat the eye using the #1 round brush and Light Grey. Paint a smaller Burnt Umber circle inside the first one for the iris, then paint the pupil Carbon Black. Add a dot of Titanium White with the tip of the brush on the upper, right section of the pupil, and three or four tiny dots on the lower, outside edge of the iris.

CACTUS

Basecoat the cactus plant and calyx with Phthalo Green, using the #8 flat brush. Using thinned Phthalo Green + Hansa Yellow (2:1) and a #3 round brush, lightly pounce highlights on the left side of cactus and top of sprouts. Allow to dry. Do the same lightly with Titanium White.

Using the same brush and Phthalo Green + Carbon Black (1: touch), pounce shadows on the right side of the cactus, bottom of each sprout and on the base of the calyx. Allow to dry, then reinforce the shadows with Phthalo Green + Carbon Black (1: touch), using the #10 flat brush.

Use the liner brush and Raw Sienna to paint the small circles that the spines grow from. Softly pounce on these circles with Raw Sienna + Titanium White (1: touch) to highlight. Paint the centers with Burnt Umber. Use the #4 flat brush and

(Continued on Page 16)

Cactus and Woodpecker
(Continued from Page 15)

Phthalo Green + Carbon Black (1: touch) to float shading around those circles.

Use the liner brush, Raw Sienna and Burnt Umber to paint spines from the circles outward. Randomly highlight the spines with lines of Titanium White.

FLOWERS

Basecoat the flowers using the #8 flat brush and Hansa Yellow + Titanium White (1: touch).

Using a #1 round brush, apply touches of thinned Titanium White randomly on the petals. Let dry, then use the mottling technique to shade the base of the petals with Hansa Yellow and Hansa Yellow + Phthalo Green.

FINISHING

For varnishing instructions, refer to "Finishing" at the front of the book.

Cactus and Woodpecker

Mabel Blanco DACA

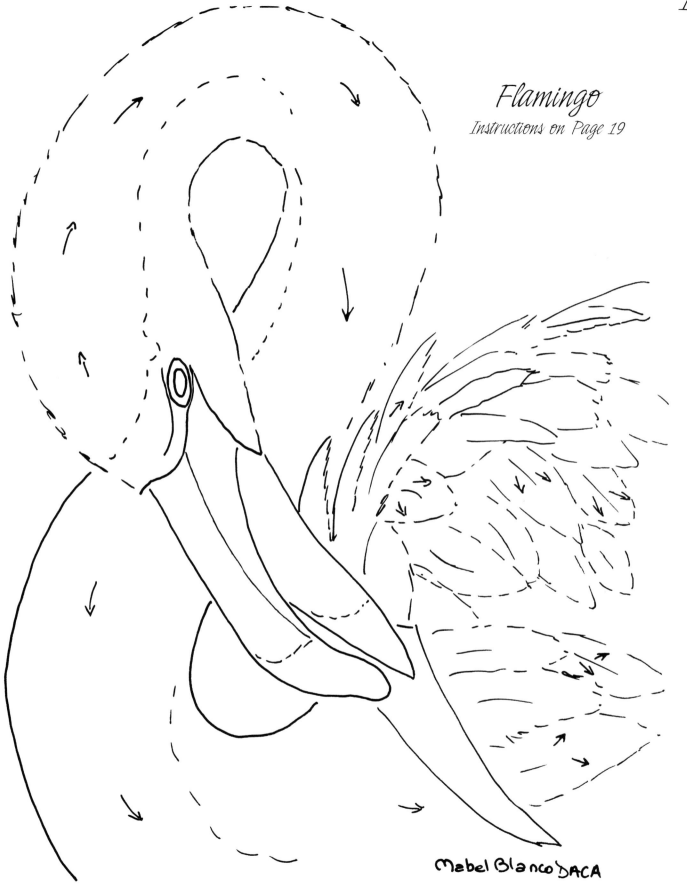

Flamingo
Instructions on Page 19

Mabel Blanco DACA

Mabel Blanco

Flamingo
Pages 17 & 19

PALETTE

DECOART
AMERICANA
ACRYLICS
Cadmium Orange
Lamp (Ebony) Black
Milk Chocolate
Primary Red
Titanium White
Ultramarine Blue
Yellow Light

SURFACE

MDF spiral-ring
book (with remov-
able spiral ring),
10" x 12" (25 x 30
cm)

BRUSHES

Liner: #10/0
Round: #1, #3
Shader: #8, #10
Wash: 1 1/2"
Worn bristle round: #6

SURFACE PREPARATION

Please refer to "Surface Preparation" at the front of the book. Remove the spiral plastic ring that holds the book together. Basecoat the front cover with Titanium White. Allow to dry, then transfer the pattern. Paint the background around the flamingo and basecoat the rest of the book with Lamp Black.

PAINTING INSTRUCTIONS

FLAMINGO

Basecoat the entire body of the flamingo (except the beak) with Cadmium Orange + Primary Red (2:1), using the #10 flat brush.

FEATHERS ON BODY: Refer to "Painting Feathers" in the General Instructions and to the color photo. The feathers on the neck are short, but in the upper, right area of the body, they are bigger and more defined.

Add a touch of Titanium White to the basecoat color and thin; use the liner brush to paint the small feathers on the head, neck and parts of the body. Let dry. Paint two more layers of feathers, adding a touch more of Titanium White to each succeeding layer. Paint Titanium White feathers on the high-light areas on the head, on the left side of the neck and in the triangular area of the neck, next to the head.

To give definition to the large, prominent feathers, drybrush around the outer edges with Milk Chocolate; allow to dry. Float Milk Chocolate over the drybrushing using the #10 flat brush.

Add a touch of Titanium White to the basecoat color and use the #3 round brush to paint the fine lines of the feathers and the central vein. Paint a few feather strokes with Titanium

White. Notice that the four standing feathers next to the neck are side views, showing the central vein on the left side and feather strokes on the right side.

Drybrush Milk Chocolate on the head, next to the beak; on the neck, where indicated with broken lines on the pattern; on the lower portion of the neck; and on the body, where it is shaded by the beak.

BEAK: Touch up the beak using a #8 flat brush and Titanium White. Allow to dry, then paint the tip of the beak and the line separating the upper and lower parts of the beak with Lamp Black.

Mix Titanium White + Lamp Black + Ultramarine Blue (1: touch: touch) and thin to ink consistency; use the #3 round brush and the mottling technique to apply this color near the face, toward the tip on the upper part, and along the separation on the bottom part.

Mix the basecoat color of the flamingo + Titanium White (1: touch) and thin; apply a wash on the lower part of the beak using the #3 round brush. Use the #10 flat brush to float the same color next to the face and along the contour line on the upper part of the beak. Using Titanium White, reinforce the highlights and paint the reflections on the black tips of the beak. Use the tip of the liner brush and Lamp Black to paint the dots on the beak as shown in the photo.

EYE: Please refer to the Eyes and Noses Color Worksheet. Paint a Titanium White oval using a #1 round brush. Allow to dry, then paint a smaller oval for the iris with Yellow Light + Lamp Black (1: touch, a greenish color). Paint the pupil with Lamp Black. Use the liner brush and thinned Lamp Black to partially outline the iris.

Use the #1 round brush to pounce Titanium White on the upper part of the iris, then soften. Use the tip of a liner brush to paint a Titanium White dot on the upper right of the pupil and five tiny dots on the lower corner of the iris.

FINISHING

For varnishing instructions, refer to "Finishing" at the front of the book.

Insert the spiral ring to attach the two pieces of the book.

Pattern on Page 17

Mabel Blanco

Beautiful Panther
Pages 21-26

PALETTE
JANSENART
TRADITIONS
ACRYLICS
Burnt Umber
Cadmium Yellow
Carbon Black
Chrome Green Hue
English Red Oxide
Hansa Yellow
Medium Grey
Perinone Orange
Raw Sienna
Titanium White
Yellow Oxide

Beautiful Panther

SURFACE
Frame, with flat
  surface, to fit panel
MDF panel, 16" x 20" (40 x 50 cm)

BRUSHES
Liner: #10/0
Round: #3
Shader: #4, #8, #12, #10, #20
Wash: 1 1/2"
Worn bristle round: #6

SPECIAL SUPPLIES
DecoArt Weathered Wood™ Crackling Medium
Pencil
Ruler

SURFACE PREPARATION
Please refer to "Surface Preparation" at the front of the book. Basecoat panel with Titanium White. Allow to dry, then transfer the pattern, omitting the spots.

PAINTING INSTRUCTIONS
BACKGROUND
Please refer to "Crisscross Strokes" at the front of the book. Using crisscross strokes and the #12 flat brush, paint the background with Chrome Green Hue, Yellow Oxide and Titanium White.

PANTHER
Please refer to the Panther Worksheet.

BASECOATING: Mix Raw Sienna + Hansa Yellow + Perinone Orange (3:1:1) for the basecoat color. Using the #8 flat brush, basecoat all areas of the animal, except the white areas around the eyes, on the muzzle and the chin. Basecoat these areas with Medium Grey. Allow to dry, then transfer the spots carefully; they give shape to the animal.

Paint the spots Carbon Black using a #4 flat brush.

HAIR: Please refer to "Painting Hair" in the front of the book. Mix basecoat color + Yellow Oxide + Perinone Orange + Titanium White (1:1:1:1). Paint several layers of hair, except on gray areas, with this color, overlapping the spots. Thin this mix, then wash over gray areas on muzzle and chin.

Add Titanium White + Yellow Oxide + Perinone Orange (1:1:1) to the last mix for a lighter color, and paint several more layers of hair.

Drybrush Burnt Umber on the left side of the panther's face, inside the ears, on the back of the ears, behind the panther's left ear, under the inner corner of the eyes, on the nose, next to the muzzle, on the body where it meets the leg, on the lower part of the leg, around the neck, in the folds and on the forehead.

Paint several layers of hair adding more of the Yellow Oxide + Perinone Orange + Titanium White mix to the previous mix each time for lighter colors. Keep the hair on the nose sparse.

On the muzzle area (not the chin), and above and below the eyes, paint several layers of hair with Titanium White. Referring to the photo, add Carbon Black hair on the top edge of both ears, back of the left ear, sparsely on the sides of the face, in the darker areas of the folds, next to the muzzle, on the white area of the muzzle, from some of the spots, and on the lower part of the leg and paw.

EARS: Inside each ear, use the basecoat color of the panther to paint short hair on outer half and along the edges. Allow to dry, then paint long hair using the basecoat color + Titanium White (1:1).

MUZZLE: Using a #4 flat brush, basecoat the nose with English Red Oxide + Titanium White (3:1). Let dry. Add Titanium White to the basecoat color and thin this mix. Use the round brush to pounce this color on the light areas around the nostrils. In the same way, add the shadows on the lower tip of the nose and along the top edge with English Red Oxide.

Use the round brush and Carbon Black to paint the area below the nostrils, the separation between the muzzle sections and the mouth. Also paint the irregular rows of spots in the whisker area above the mouth.

Use a liner brush and thinned Titanium White to paint long whiskers on the muzzle. Paint a few long hairs above the eyes.

Use the liner brush and thinned Titanium White to paint two layers of short hair on the chin; let dry, then paint longer hair. Add a few hairs with Medium Grey. Using Carbon Black and the tip of the liner brush, apply tiny dots on the dark area under the mouth.

EYES: Refer to the Eyes and Noses Color Worksheet. Use the round brush and Carbon Black to paint the area around each eye. Basecoat each iris with Hansa Yellow + Carbon Black (4:1), a greenish color. Add a touch of Titanium White to the mix, then use the round brush to paint a comma stroke on the lower edge of the iris, then soften. Using the mottling technique, add Titanium White to the previous mix and highlight the lower part of the iris. Allow to dry, then repeat with Cadmium Yellow.

Paint the pupil with Carbon Black. Using the #10 flat brush, float Carbon Black shading on the top of the iris, where the eyelid projects a shadow. Using the round brush and thinned

(Continued on Page 22)

Beautiful Panther
(Continued from Page 21)

of the eye, from the corner to just inside the pupil. Allow to dry, then place a dot of Titanium White on the pupil where the soft highlight ends.

Paint a very fine line of thinned Titanium White below the iris, following the shape of the eye. Place another line in the inner corner of the eye, softening the color outward. Allow to dry, then reinforce the highlight with Titanium White. Use the liner brush and thinned Titanium White to paint the eyelashes.

ROCK

Basecoat with Medium Grey using the #12 flat brush. Allow to dry.

Refer to "Mottling" in the front of the book. Drop Titanium White + Raw Sienna (3:1) over the surface of the rock. Repeat with Burnt Umber and Raw Sienna. When dry, float shading using the #10 flat brush and Burnt Umber. Let dry and repeat the mottling to reinforce the effect. Finally, drop some Carbon Black to reinforce shadows.

FRAME

Using the wash brush and thinned Raw Sienna, paint the frame. To avoid leaving brush marks, pull each stroke the length of a section of the frame without lifting. Allow to dry.

Measure five inches from the outer corner on all sides and mark. Paint the corners inside the marks with Raw Sienna, using the #20 flat brush. Let dry.

Use the #20 flat brush to apply crackling medium on the corners, then let dry for 60 minutes. Paint over the corners with Titanium White + Raw Sienna (3:1) using short strokes. When dry, paint thinned Burnt Umber over this, then wipe excess paint to achieve a weathered appearance.

FINISHING

For varnishing instructions, refer to "Finishing" at the front of the book.

Beautiful Panther

Match and attach with the pattern
section on pages 24-25

Beautiful Panther
Instructions on Pages 21-22

Match and attach with the pattern
section on pages 22-23

DACA

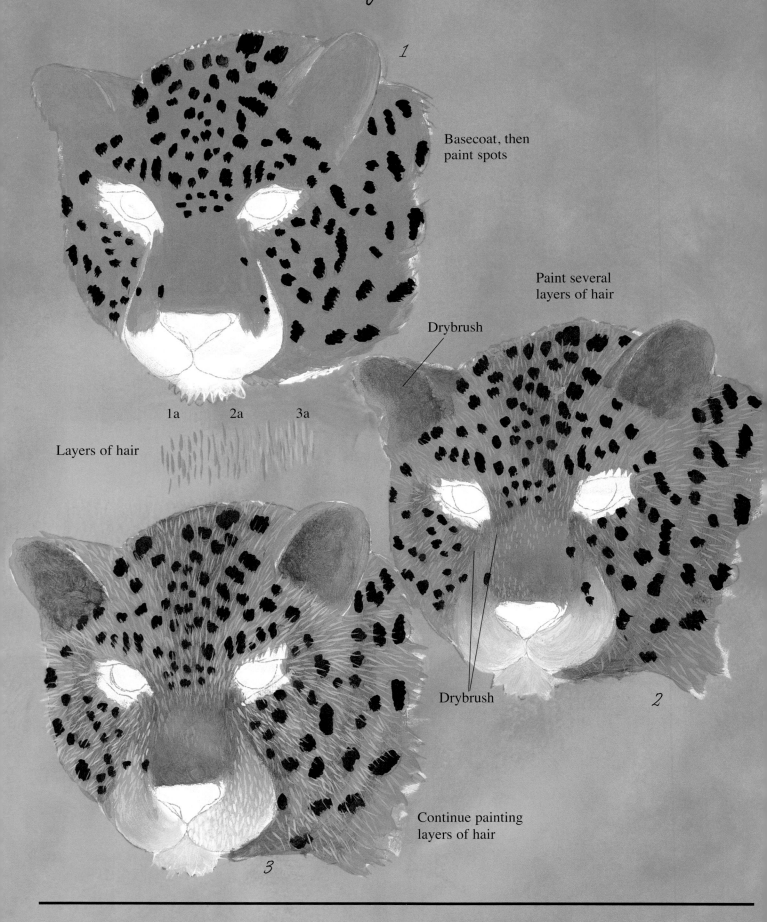

1

Basecoat, then
paint spots

Paint several
layers of hair

Drybrush

1a   2a   3a

Layers of hair

Drybrush

2

Continue painting
layers of hair

3

Color Photo on Page 29

PALETTE
DECOART AMERICANA ACRYLICS
Antique Gold
Bright Orange
Burnt Sienna
Burnt Umber
Kelly Green
Lamp (Ebony) Black
Midnite Blue
Mistletoe
Moon Yellow
Primary Red
Primary Yellow
Titanium White
Ultramarine Blue
Vivid Violet
DECOART AMERICANA DAZZLING METALLICS
Glorious Gold

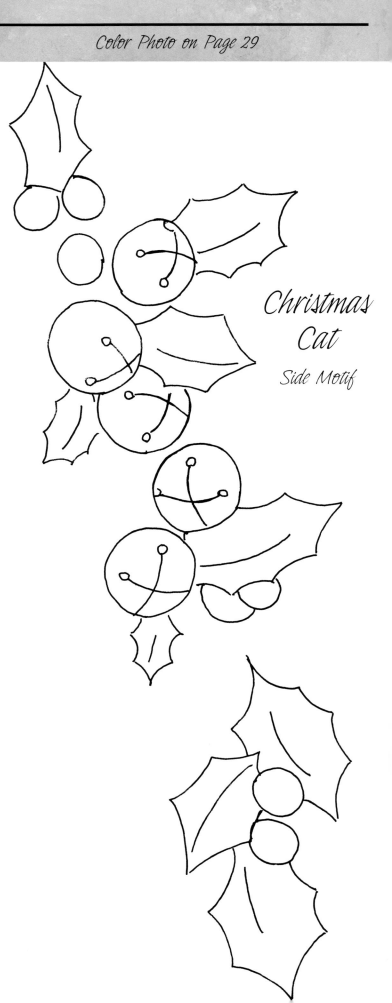

Christmas Cat

Christmas Cat
Side Motif

SURFACE
Wine box, 9"W x 14"T x 4 1/2"D (23 x 35.5 x 11.5 cm)

BRUSHES
Liner: #10/0
Round: #1, #3
Shader: #3, #6, #8, #10, #16
Stencil: #8
Wash: 1 1/2"
Worn bristle round: #6

SPECIAL SUPPLIES
DecoArt Star Lite Topcoat™
Masking tape
Star stencil, 1/2"

SURFACE PREPARATION
Please refer to "Surface Preparation" in the General Instructions. Basecoat the box, inside and out, with Titanium White. Allow to dry, then transfer the patterns.

Using the wash brush and Vivid Violet, paint the inside of the box and the back of the box. Allow to dry.

PAINTING INSTRUCTIONS
BACKGROUND
Using the #16 flat brush, basecoat the table with Lamp Black. Basecoat the remainder of the background and the rest of the box with Midnite Blue.

CHRISTMAS BOX
Using the #10 flat brush and Kelly Green, basecoat the box and allow to dry. Tape the stencil in place on the box; place tape on one side so you can lift the stencil to check if corrections are needed. Load your dry stencil brush with Glorious Gold. Wipe the excess paint on a paper towel, then touch the bristles lightly; if the bristles feel dry, the brush has been properly prepared. Applying very little pressure, start moving your

(Continued on Page 30)

Christmas Cat
Pages 27-28 & 30

Christmas Cat
(Continued from Page 28)

brush with a circular motion over the stencil; start on the mylar and slowly move over the openings. Continue slowly moving across the stars using a circular motion, until you complete all the stars. Check to see if corrections are needed before removing stencil.

Using the #10 flat brush, float Lamp Black on the edges of the left panel of the box and below the tissue. On the left edge, walk the shading further toward the right.

On the right panel of the box, float Titanium White on the left edge (at the corner).

Using the stylus and Glorious Gold, make a border of dots along the bottom of the box.

PAPER

Basecoat the paper with Primary Red using the #10 flat brush. Let dry. Using the same brush, drybrush the shaded areas with Primary Red + Lamp Black (1: touch). Use the same brush and Lamp Black to strengthen the shading. Using Moon Yellow, float along the edges to highlight, then strengthen the highlight on the left side using a liner brush.

JINGLE BELLS

Basecoat the bells using the #6 flat brush and Antique Gold. Float Burnt Sienna on the left side of each bell. Let dry. Float Burnt Umber to reinforce the shadows.

Use the #3 round brush and Burnt Umber to paint the holes on each bell; start with the dots, then paint the lines. Use the liner brush and Titanium White to highlight the holes. Outline the bells with Burnt Umber.

BERRIES

On the front of the box, use the end of a brush handle loaded with Primary Red to apply a dot for each berry, two or three in each group.

Basecoat the berries on the sides of the box with Primary Red. Pounce first with Bright Orange, then with Primary Yellow to shape and highlight. Add a few tiny Titanium White dots to strengthen the highlight. Shade with Burnt Umber.

LEAVES

Basecoat the leaves on the front of the box using a #3 flat brush and Mistletoe. Paint the central vein with a liner brush and Burnt Umber. Using a #8 flat brush, float Titanium White + Moon Yellow (2:1) on the light areas of the leaf and Burnt Umber on the dark areas.

Basecoat the leaves on the side of the box with Kelly Green. Highlight with Kelly Green + Titanium White (1: touch). Shade with Burnt Umber. Use the liner brush and Titanium White to paint the veins and to randomly outline the leaves.

CAT

Using a #6 flat brush, basecoat the black areas with Lamp Black. Basecoat the light areas (not the ears) with Titanium White + Lamp Black (1: touch). Basecoat inside the ears with Titanium White + Burnt Sienna (3:1).

Drybrush Titanium White + Lamp Black (4:1) shading on the left side of the face, on both sides of the muzzle, in the folds of the neck, on top and side of left leg, on right leg next to chest, on the chest, and inside the ears on the inner edge and bottom. Use the #10 flat brush to float the same color under the eyes.

Refer to "Painting Hair" in the General Instructions. This cat has short thin hair. Paint one layer of hair in the black areas with Titanium White + Ultramarine Blue (3:1).

On the gray areas, paint a layer of hair with Titanium White + Lamp Black (1: touch). Let dry, then apply two layers of hair with Titanium White. Float Titanium White + Burnt Sienna (2:1) to separate the toes.

MUZZLE: With the #6 flat brush, float Titanium White + Burnt Sienna (2:1) around the sides of the nose and above the mouth. Using the same mix and the #3 flat brush, basecoat the nose. Add a touch of Titanium White to this mix to highlight the nose around the nostrils. Using the liner brush and Burnt Sienna, paint the nostrils, the line below the nose and the line of the mouth. Using the #1 round brush, softly pounce Burnt Sienna on the base of the nose.

Using a #6 flat brush, float Titanium White + Lamp Black (1:1) on the mouth line. Using a liner brush and the same color, paint dots on the muzzle. Using a liner brush, pull strokes for whiskers with thinned Titanium White, then pull a stroke with thinned Titanium White + Lamp Black (4:1) under each whisker.

EYES: Outline the eyes with a #3 round brush and Lamp Black. Basecoat the irises with Titanium White + Ultramarine Blue (4:1). With the tip of the brush and Lamp Black, paint a vertical oval in the center of each iris. When dry, use Lamp Black to shade the top of the eye. Add more Titanium White to the iris basecoat mix and thin. Using the #3 round brush, apply dots on the lower part of each iris. Let dry. Repeat both steps to reinforce the color.

Use the liner brush and thinned Titanium White to paint a line from the pupil into the iris on the upper, right side, then soften. Let dry, then reinforce the highlight with a Titanium White dot.

Paint the line next to the outer side of each iris (in the black area) and the tiny spot in the corner of the eye with thinned Titanium White, using a liner brush.

EARS: Paint thin, short hairs inside the ears, using the liner brush and thinned Titanium White. With the same brush and color, paint the long hairs, starting from the edge and pulling inward.

FINISHING

Using the #10 flat brush, apply Star Lite Topcoat over the blue area of the box cover. Allow to dry. Refer to "Finishing" in the General Instructions and varnish the rest of the box. Attach rope handle.

Remaining Pattern on Page 27

Puma

Color Photo on Page 31

Puma

PALETTE
JANSENART
TRADITIONS
ACRYLICS
Burnt Sienna
Burnt Umber
Carbon Black
Chrome Green Hue
English Red Oxide
Hansa Yellow
Indian Yellow
Light Grey Value 8
Medium Grey
Raw Sienna
Raw Umber
Titanium White

SURFACE
Canvas or wooden board, 16" x 20" (40 x 50 cm)
Frame to fit canvas

BRUSHES
Liner: #1
Round: #1, #3
Shader: #4, #6, #10, #20
Wash: 1 1/2"
Worn bristle round: #6

SPECIAL SUPPLIES
DecoArt Americana Acrylic Sealer/Finisher, matte (DAS13)
Dick Blick Gold Leafing Antiquing Kit (#841)

SURFACE PREPARATION
Please refer to "Surface Preparation" at the front of the book. Basecoat canvas with Titanium White. Allow to dry, then transfer the basic outlines of the pattern; transfer the details as you need them.

PAINTING INSTRUCTIONS
BACKGROUND
Please refer to "Crisscross Strokes" at the front of the book. Using crisscross strokes and the #10 flat brush, paint the background with Chrome Green Hue, Carbon Black, Titanium White and Hansa Yellow, leaving the colors more defined than on the backgrounds of the other projects. Allow to dry. Using the same technique and brush, highlight some areas with Hansa Yellow or Titanium White. Allow to dry. Again using the same technique and brush, apply Burnt Sienna, English Red Oxide and Titanium White with loose strokes to paint an undefined bush on the left.

STONE
Using the #20 flat brush, basecoat the stone with Light Grey and allow to dry. Refer to "Mottling" in the General Instructions. Using the #3 round brush, mottle first with Titanium White, then with Medium Grey and Raw Sienna. Let dry, then continue to work in the same way with Chrome Green Hue and Burnt Sienna. Allow to dry.

Using the #3 round brush and Titanium White, pounce patches of snow on the surface of the rock, allowing the color to show more in some areas than in others. Using the liner brush and Carbon Black, loosely outline under each clump of snow to shade.

PUMA
Basecoat the brown areas of the puma with Raw Sienna + Titanium White + Carbon Black (4:1: touch). Basecoat the light areas on the feet, leg, chest, muzzle and chin, around the eyes and on the edges of the ears with Light Grey.

Refer to the color photo and drybrush Burnt Sienna on the tip of the tail; on the shadow projected on the tail by the hind leg; on the hind legs, including under the chest; between the front legs; along the round line of the belly; in the depressions on the body created by the muscles and bones; the separation between the head and the body; on the top of the head; on the nose, and between the nose and the eyes; on the muzzle; and at the sides of the eyes.

Reinforce the shadows by drybrushing Burnt Umber on the tip of the tail and next to the leg, under the belly, on the legs, on the cheeks, in the creases above the eyes and on the muzzle. Repeat the drybrushing after painting hair to reinforce as necessary.

Refer to "Painting Hair" in the General Instructions. Add a touch of Indian Yellow to the basecoat mix and thin; paint a layer of hair on the brown areas in the direction indicated on the pattern. The hair should be short and stiff.

Add another touch of Indian Yellow to the previous color and paint another layer of hair. Allow to dry, then paint another layer of hair with thinned Burnt Sienna, concentrating this layer in the shadow areas. Don't worry, the paint is diluted with water so you won't cover the previous work.

To strengthen the dark areas, use the liner brush and Raw Umber to paint hair on these areas. Paint the yellow hair (reflected light) on the right side of the face and chest with Hansa Yellow.

Using the liner brush and Titanium White, paint several layers of hair on the white areas of the leg, feet, muzzle, chin, over and under the eyes, on the edges of the ears and on the chest. Use the #10 flat brush to float Light Grey + Titanium White (1: touch) in the separations between the toes and on the chest below the head.

EARS: Basecoat the inside of the ears using the #10 flat brush and Titanium White + English Red Oxide (3:1). Float Burnt Umber lightly around the edges and on the bottom of each ear for depth. Using thinned Titanium White, paint small, fine hairs inside the ears, trying not to cover the entire surface, then paint the longer

(Continued on Page 34)

Puma

Match and attach with the pattern
section on pages 34-35

Puma
(Continued from Page 32)

hair. Use the colors of the hair on the rest of the puma to pull some hair up over the ears from the face.

EYES: Refer to the Eyes and Noses Color Worksheet. Paint the outline of the eyes with a #1 round brush and Carbon Black. Using the #3 round brush and Hansa Yellow + Carbon Black (4:1), paint the irises. Paint the pupils Carbon Black.

Using a #6 flat brush, float Carbon Black along the top of each eye. Add some Titanium White to the iris basecoat color and float on the lower edge of each iris. Using the same mix and the #3 round brush, paint a comma stroke on the bottom of each iris, then soften.

Add a highlight to each eye using the #1 round brush and Titanium White, then soften. Reinforce the highlight with a dot of Titanium White. Use Titanium White to paint the line below the iris (in the black area) and the highlight in the inner corner of each eye.

Using the liner brush, paint eyelashes with thinned Titanium White + Hansa Yellow (2:1).

MUZZLE: Basecoat the nose with English Red Oxide + Titanium White (1: touch), using the #6 flat brush. Pounce the same mix + Burnt Umber (1: touch) on the nose. Outline the nose and mouth using the #1 round brush and Carbon Black.

Using a #4 flat brush and thinned Burnt Umber, reinforce the dark areas around the white area of the muzzle, and the two dark markings over the eyes, where the nose ends on the forehead. Using the tip of the liner brush and Carbon Black, paint three rows of dots on each side of the muzzle in the white areas.

The whiskers are painted with thinned Titanium White and Carbon Black strokes painted side by side. Start at the dots and pull outward.

SNOW
Once you have finished painting, splatter the painting with Titanium White to simulate the falling snow.

FRAME
Using the #20 flat brush, paint a wash of Raw Sienna over the frame. Allow to dry. Mark 3 1/4" in from the outer corner along each side and mark. Following the instructions for gold leafing on the kit, gild the corners of the frame.

FINISHING
For varnishing instructions, refer to "Finishing" at the front of the book.

Puma

Match and attach with the pattern
section on pages 32-33

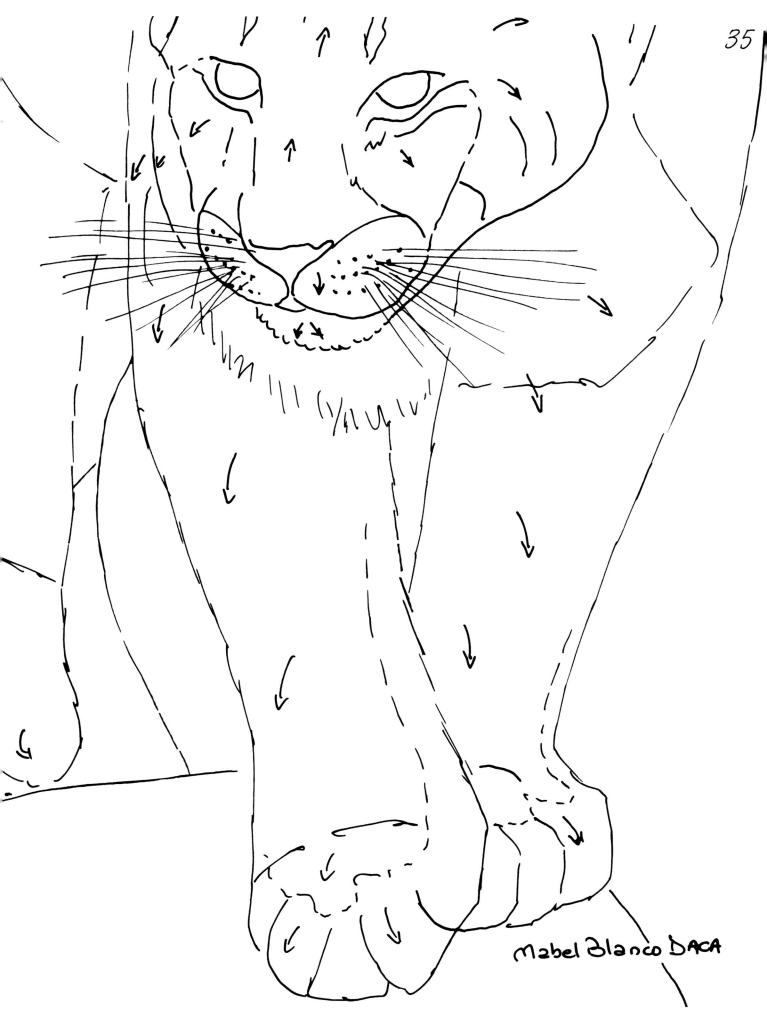

Mabel Blanco DACA

Mabel Blanco

Chunky
Pages 37-38

PALETTE
DECOART
AMERICANA
ACRYLICS
Antique Gold
Burnt Sienna
Burnt Umber
Calypso Blue
Lamp (Ebony) Black
Raw Sienna
Sable Brown
Titanium White
Ultramarine Blue

Chunky

SURFACE
MDF box, 8" x 8" (20.5 x 20.5 cm)

BRUSHES
Liner: #10/0
Round: #3
Shader: #6, #10, #20
Stencil: #8
Wash: 1 1/2"
Worn bristle round: #6 (several)

SPECIAL SUPPLIES
Masking tape
Paw stencil or supplies for cutting a stencil

SURFACE PREPARATION
Please refer to "Surface Preparation" at the front of the book. Basecoat the box and lid with Titanium White. Use the #6 flat brush and Sable Brown to paint the routed edge of the lid. Allow to dry, then transfer the pattern.

PAINTING INSTRUCTIONS
BACKGROUND
Using #20 flat brush, basecoat the background behind the cat and the box with Calypso Blue + Titanium White (2:1).

CAT
Using the #6 flat brush and Lamp Black, basecoat the ears, the paw and the area between the eyes. Basecoat the rest of the head with Titanium White + Lamp Black (4:1) and let dry.

Drybrush Raw Sienna between the eyes, on both sides of the face and muzzle, on the chin and along the face where it rests on the basket.

Please refer to "Painting Hair" in the General Instructions. On this cat, the hair is shorter in the middle of the face but is longer on the rest of the head. Paint the hair in the direction indicated by the arrows on the pattern. Paint the whiskers and the hair on the paw after painting the basket.

Using a liner brush and Lamp Black, paint hair on the edges of the ears, between the eyes, on both sides of the muzzle, and on the sides and bottom of the paw. Allow to dry, then paint the first layer of hair on the rest of the head with Titanium White.

Using a #10 flat brush, float Raw Sienna above the black area between the eyes, next to the outer edges of the eyes, on the area below the nose, above the paw and on the chin where it rests on the basket.

Paint two more layers of hair with Titanium White, making it long and flowing. The hair on the chin curves to the left. Add the longer hair to ears with Titanium White.

Paint some longer hair with Lamp Black between the eyes, overlapping the white hair. Paint some short hair in this area and down onto the muzzle with Titanium White. Add some hair to the head with Titanium White + Burnt Sienna (1: touch).

Paint short hair with Raw Sienna + Burnt Sienna (1: touch) on both sides of the muzzle, on the paw and chin, above and on the black area between the eyes, and on edges of ears. Add short hair on the claw area and left side of the paw with Titanium White.

NOSE: Using a liner brush, outline the nose and the mouth line with Lamp Black, then use a #6 flat brush and the same color to basecoat the nose. Let dry.

Refer to "Mottling" in the front of the book, then load a #3 round brush with Titanium White and use the technique to highlight the nose. Let dry and pull strokes for whiskers using the liner brush and Lamp Black.

EYES: Please refer to the Eyes and Noses Color Worksheet. Outline the shape of the eyes using the #3 round brush and Lamp Black. Use the same brush and Titanium White + Ultramarine Blue (3:1) to basecoat the irises.

With a #3 round brush and Lamp Black, paint the pupils. Let dry, then use the same brush and color, and the mottling technique to shade the upper part of each iris, following the shape of the eye. Let dry and use the same technique to highlight the lower part of the iris with Titanium White. If necessary, repeat to reinforce highlights on the bottom of the iris and on both sides of the pupil.

Using the same brush, paint two tiny dots at each side of the pupil and dots on the bottom of the iris with Titanium White to enhance light reflection.

BASKET
LOWER PART: Using a #6 flat brush, basecoat all woven sections (horizontal and vertical) with Burnt Sienna and let dry. Using the same brush, float Burnt Umber on the top and bottom of the vertical sections, and on the horizontal sections next to the vertical ones. Load the same brush with Antique Gold + Titanium White (3:1), then use the chisel edge to stroke back and forth to create the texture on the middle of both the vertical and horizontal sections. Allow to dry.

Add a touch of Titanium White to the previous mix, and then use the same technique to highlight the central area of the horizontal sections. Use a liner brush and thinned Burnt Sienna to outline the sections.

RIM AND HANDLE: Basecoat the wicker with Burnt Sienna using the #6 flat brush. Using the liner brush and

(Continued on Page 38)

Chunky
(Continued from Page 37)

thinned Lamp Black, outline the sections. Then, with a #10 flat brush, float Burnt Umber shading on the lower edge.

Highlight these sections like the woven sections of the basket, stroking vertically instead of horizontally.

Basecoat the knob at the end of the handle with Burnt Sienna. Highlight the knob with Antique Gold + Titanium White (3:1), then use a #10 flat brush and Burnt Umber to float shading along the bottom.

METAL RING: Using the #3 round brush, basecoat the ring with Titanium White + Lamp Black (3:1). Let dry. Using the same mix + Titanium White (1: touch), paint tiny dots over the surface. Let dry, then paint Titanium White dots toward the top and Lamp Black dots toward the bottom. Outline with Lamp Black. Paint the hole the ring passes through with Burnt Umber.

PAW PRINTS

Please refer to the stenciling instructions in the "Christmas Box" section of the Christmas Cat project. Stencil the paw prints on the sides of the box with Sable Brown.

FINISHING

For varnishing instructions, refer to "Finishing" at the front of the book.

Side Motif

Chunky

Mabel Blanco DACA

PALETTE
DECOART AMERICANA ACRYLICS
Alizarin Crimson
Antique Gold
Bright Orange
Burnt Sienna
Burnt Umber
Cadmium Yellow
Lamp (Ebony) Black
Mistletoe
Moon Yellow
Napthol Red
Payne's Grey
Royal Fuchsia
Sand
Titanium White

SURFACE
Frame to fit panel
MDF panel, 10" x 12" (25 x 30 cm)

BRUSHES
Liner: #10/0
Round: #1, #3
Shader: #4, #6, #8, #10
Wash: 1 1/2"
Worn bristle round: #6

SURFACE PREPARATION

Please refer to "Surface Preparation" at the front of the book. Basecoat the design panel with Titanium White. Allow to dry, then transfer the basic outlines of the pattern; transfer the details as needed.

PAINTING INSTRUCTIONS
BACKGROUND

Please refer to "Crisscross Strokes" at the front of the book. Using the crisscross strokes and the #8 flat brush, paint the background with Mistletoe, Moon Yellow and Lamp Black. Let dry.

Using a #6 flat brush and crisscross strokes, paint the area around the toucan with Moon Yellow + Mistletoe (2:1) to suggest the background foliage.

BRANCH

Basecoat the branch with Burnt Sienna using the #8 flat brush. Clean the brush and load with thinned Antique Gold. Apply paint along the branch using the chisel edge of the brush and short, irregular strokes to add texture. Float Burnt Umber to shade the bottom of the branch and around the feet. Use the #3 round brush to paint short, irregular lines with Antique Gold + Titanium White + Burnt Sienna (2:1:1). Use the liner brush and Lamp Black to outline the dark edge of the branch.

TOUCAN

Using the #8 flat brush, basecoat the black areas of the toucan's body and tail with Lamp Black; the red area with Napthol Red, adding a touch of Lamp Black toward the bottom;

Toucan and Orchids

the yellow area of the chest with Cadmium Yellow; and the red area around the eye with Napthol Red (use the chisel edge of the brush and short, choppy strokes).

Paint the feet using a #3 round brush and Titanium White + Lamp Black (4:1).

Paint the black area of the beak with a #8 flat brush and Lamp Black. Use the chisel edge of the #4 flat brush and horizontal strokes to paint the light area of the beak with thinned Sand + Titanium White + Antique Gold (1:1:1). The beak should have an uneven texture.

Refer to "Painting Feathers" in the General Instructions. On the black areas, paint feathers with thinned Payne's Grey + Titanium White (1: touch), starting at the head and following the shape of the bird as indicated in the pattern.

In the yellow area, drybrush Napthol Red on the left side and lower, right side (refer to color photo), then paint a layer of feathers on the entire area with Cadmium Yellow + Titanium White (1: touch). Using Napthol Red + Bright Orange + Cadmium Yellow (1:1:1), paint feathers along the left side and on the lower, right side of the yellow area. Also paint some feathers on the red area around the eye. Drybrush Titanium White + Cadmium Yellow (1: touch) under the orange ring around the eye to highlight that area.

Paint irregular feathers with Titanium White on the left side and bottom of the yellow area with the liner brush.

Paint a layer of Cadmium Yellow + Bright Orange (1:1) feathers on the lighter part of the red area and Napthol Red + Lamp Black (2:1) feathers on the darker part. Drybrush the bottom portion of the dark area with Lamp Black.

EYE: Refer to the Eyes and Noses Color Worksheet. Paint an oval using a #1 round brush and Titanium White + Lamp Black (3:1). Inside the oval, paint a smaller oval (the iris) with Sand + Mistletoe (2:1). Using the liner brush, outline the iris and eye with Lamp Black. Using the tip of the brush, paint a Lamp Black dot in the center of the iris.

Using the #4 flat brush, float Lamp Black along the top of each eye. Add highlight dots with Titanium White on the right edge of the pupil and below the right side of the iris.

BEAK: Using the #10 flat brush, float Burnt Sienna to separate the lower and upper sections. Float the same color on the upper, left edge of the upper section. Float Titanium White above the separation line on the upper section.

Drybrush Titanium White on the lightest areas of the upper section. Refer to "Mottling," then use the #3 round brush and Payne's Grey to highlight the black area.

TOES: To separate the toes, outline with Lamp Black using the liner brush. To create form, paint lines around the toes with Titanium White + Lamp Black (1: touch) and Lamp Black, using the #1 round brush. Use the liner brush and Lamp Black to paint the nails, then highlight with Titanium White strokes.

ORCHIDS
PETALS: Using the #4 flat brush, basecoat the orange petals with Cadmium Yellow + Bright Orange + Napthol Red

(Continued on Page 40)

Toucan and Orchids
Pages 39-41

Toucan and Orchids
(Continued from Page 39)

(2:1:1), and the edge of the folded petal with Cadmium Yellow + Napthol Red (1:1). Pounce the highlight areas with Titanium White + Cadmium Yellow (2:1). Pounce the mid-value areas with Cadmium Yellow and the shadow areas with Cadmium Yellow + Napthol Red (2:1).

Using a #3 round brush and Royal Fuchsia + Titanium White (1: touch), paint the center petal of each flower. Use the #10 flat brush to float Titanium White on the edge of the petal. Use the #3 round brush and Royal Fuchsia + Alizarin Crimson to paint the central area of the flower. Allow to dry, then paint the strokes in the center of the left flower with Cadmium Yellow.

LEAVES: Basecoat the leaves with Mistletoe using the #8 flat brush. Using the #10 flat brush, float Mistletoe + Lamp Black (1: touch) to shade and Moon Yellow + Mistletoe (2:1) to highlight. Allow to dry, then randomly outline the petals and center petal of the flowers with Lamp Black.

FINISHING

For varnishing instructions, refer to "Finishing" at the front of the book.

Toucan and
Orchids

Mabel Blanco DACA

PALETTE

JANSENART
TRADITIONS
ACRYLICS
Burnt Sienna
Burnt Umber
Carbon Black
Chrome Green Hue
Perinone Orange
Pine Green
Raw Sienna
Titanium White
Yellow Oxide

Little Wolf

SURFACE

Round tray or surface
with 9 3/4" design
area (25 cm)

BRUSHES

Liner: #10/0
Round: #2, #3, #5
Shader: #8, #10, #12
Wash: 1 1/2"
Worn bristle round: #6

SURFACE PREPARATION

Please refer to "Surface Preparation" at the front of the book. Basecoat the design area with Titanium White. Allow to dry, then transfer the pattern, omitting the small foreground branches and leaves.

PAINTING INSTRUCTIONS
BACKGROUND

Please refer to "Crisscross Strokes" at the front of the book. Using crisscross strokes and the #12 flat brush, paint the background with Pine Green and Carbon Black.

To paint the more distant leaves that fade into the background, mix Pine Green + Yellow Oxide (1:1). Load the #5 round brush with this color, place the tip on the surface, lean the brush to the side, press to flatten the bristles, slide and lift. Cover the background with leaves. Add a touch more Yellow Oxide to the mix, then lightly highlight the leaves. Use Pine Green to randomly outline leaves as necessary for definition.

TREE TRUNK

Use a #8 flat brush to basecoat the trunk with Burnt Umber. Let dry. Using the #2 round brush and Carbon Black, paint the center crevice. Use thinned Titanium White + Yellow Oxide (1:1) to paint the smaller crevices next to it and to form the shaggy bark.

Using a liner brush and Yellow Oxide, paint broken strokes to form bark along the top edge of the trunk. Allow to dry, then paint a wash of Burnt Sienna over the trunk. Use the #3 round brush and Carbon Black to paint the shaded area where the wolf rests his chin.

WOLF

Use a #6 flat brush and Raw Sienna + Perinone Orange + Yellow Oxide (3:1:1) to basecoat the head (except the chin) and inside the ears. Allow to dry, then basecoat the chin with Burnt Umber.

Drybrush Burnt Sienna on the inner edge of the top of the ears, in the folds on both sides of the muzzle and next to the eyes, and under the eyes. Drybrush Burnt Umber in some of the folds to deepen the shading.

Drybrush inside the ears with Titanium White + Burnt Sienna (3:1).

To begin painting the hair, mix the basecoat color with a touch of Yellow Oxide and thin. Paint a layer of hair on the head, but do not apply to the inside of the ears and the chin. Lighten the basecoat color with more Yellow Oxide and paint another layer in the same areas. Paint Burnt Sienna hair along the top of the head, on both sides of each eye, and along the edges of the muzzle, on the chin and on the tip of each ear.

Drybrush Burnt Umber over the nose (between the eyes) and around the mouth. Using Yellow Oxide + Titanium White (1: touch), paint the light hair over and under the eyes, and under the nose.

Drybrush Burnt Umber inside the ears to add depth. Use Titanium White + Burnt Sienna (2:1) and the liner brush to paint the short hair inside the ears. Using Titanium White, paint hair on the outer edge of the ears, then paint the long hair inside the ears.

EYES: Please refer to the Eyes and Noses Color Worksheet. Paint the outline around the eyes with the #3 round brush and Carbon Black. Paint the irises with Burnt Umber. Paint the pupils with Carbon Black. Use the #3 round brush and thinned Yellow Oxide + Burnt Umber (3:1) to paint a comma stroke in the lower part of each iris, then soften. Use Titanium White to float a reflection at the top of the eye, then reinforce with a dot of Titanium White. Also add tiny dots with the tip of the bristles on the black on the lower eyelid, and in the inner corner of each eye. Paint tiny eyelashes with Titanium White.

MUZZLE: Using Carbon Black and the #3 round brush, basecoat the nose, then outline the mouth. Use the same brush and thinned Titanium White dots to shape the nose and nostrils. Paint inside the nostrils with Carbon Black. Use the liner brush and Titanium White for the highlights on the nose and mouth.

Using the tip of the liner brush, paint three rows of tiny Carbon Black dots on each side of the muzzle. Paint whiskers with thinned Burnt Sienna, then highlight with strokes of Titanium White.

BRANCHES AND LEAVES IN FOREGROUND

Basecoat the branches using the #3 round brush and Burnt Umber. Let dry. Using the same brush and Titanium White + Yellow Oxide (1:1), paint short strokes down the branch to add texture and highlights.

Paint the leaves with the #5 round brush and Chrome Green Hue, using the same method you used for painting the background leaves.